This book belongs to

Made in the USA
Monee, IL
21 April 2022

95127236R00061